D0753324

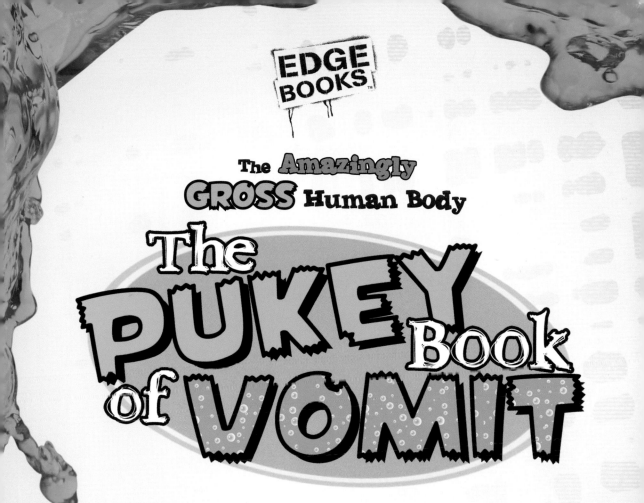

EDGE BOOKS™

The Amazingly GROSS Human Body

The PUKEY Book of VOMIT

By Connie Colwell Miller

Consultant:
Michael Bentley
Professor of Biology
Minnesota State University
Mankato, Minnesota

Capstone press®

Mankato, Minnesota

Edge Books are published by Capstone Press,
151 Good Counsel Drive, P.O. Box 669, Mankato, Minnesota 56002.
www.capstonepress.com

Library of Congress Cataloging-in-Publication Data
Miller, Connie Colwell, 1976–
    The pukey book of vomit / by Connie Colwell Miller.
    p. cm. — (Edge. The amazingly gross human body)
    Summary: "Describes what vomit consists of, how the human body
manufactures vomit, and why vomit is gross" — Provided by publisher.
    Includes bibliographical references and index.
    ISBN 978-1-4296-3356-7 (library binding)
    1. Vomiting — Juvenile literature. 2. Nausea — Juvenile literature. I. Title.
II. Series.
RB150.N38M55 2010
616'.047 — dc22   2009002166

Editorial Credits
Mandy Robbins, editor; Kyle Grenz, designer; Jo Miller, media researcher

Photo Credits
Capstone Press/Karon Dubke, cover, 4, 7 (both), 8, 10 (inset), 12, 14, 15, 17, 18,
    19, 25 (main image), 26, 29 (inset)
Department of Defense, 21
Getty Images Inc./UpperCut Images/Keith Brofsky, 20
Photo Researchers, Inc/John Bavosi, 10–11; Mark Clarke, 22
Shutterstock/Adrian Hughes, 29 (rat); Filipe B. Varela (pouring water design
    element), throughout; JR Trice, 25 (peppermints); Oguz Aral, 23

TABLE of CONTENTS

VOMIT'S Nasty STORY

Nausea is that feeling you get just before you vomit.

You've been spending the day with your cousin, who just got over the stomach flu. Suddenly you're not feeling so well. Your stomach is **churning**. There's a strange taste in your mouth. You know what's coming next.

That's right — vomit, barf, puke, upchuck, hurl. Whatever word you use to describe it, vomiting is a rather disgusting fact of life.

But there's more to vomit than you think. Vomiting is your body's way of shoving out stuff that could make you even sicker than you already feel. Read on to learn more about the putrid, yet practical, story of puke.

 churn to move violently; when the contents of your stomach churn, you feel sick.

THE TRUTH ABOUT PUKE

Vomit is the gross mix of food and stomach juices that shoots out of your mouth from time to time. Most people know that vomit is made of whatever they have recently eaten. But it's also made of stomach **acids** and a slimy, green substance called **bile**.

Even though it feels horrible, vomiting is often a good thing. Most people think that vomiting means you're sick. But that's not always the case. Throwing up is also your body's way of protecting you. Sometimes your body wants you to barf because you've eaten something that might cause it harm.

acid — a strong liquid that helps break down food into energy

bile — a green liquid made by the liver and released into the intestines; bile helps digest food.

When you vomit, your stomach turns almost completely inside out.

What could be more gross than sticking your head into a toilet and vomiting?

HOW VOMIT HAPPENS

The urge to vomit is impossible to control.

Just about everyone has thrown up. But how does it happen? What is the process that your body goes through when you eat? And just what happens when your food comes back up?

WHAT'S SUPPOSED TO HAPPEN

Most of the time, chewed-up food slides down your throat and into your stomach. There, acids and **enzymes** start breaking down food into energy and nutrients your body can use.

Your food continues to break down as it moves through your **intestines**. Leftover food leaves your body as waste, or poop.

Of course, that's what happens when everything is working well. But sometimes, what goes down must come back up.

enzyme   a substance that helps break down food

intestines   a long tube below the stomach that digests food and absorbs liquids and salts

9

THE BARF CYCLE

Your body is smart. It knows what does and does not belong inside it. When something gets into your body that shouldn't be there, your brain sends signals to get rid of it as soon as possible.

The vomiting center in your brain is in charge of making you throw up. This part of your brain sends signals all over your body, telling it to get ready to barf.

vomit's path

GROSS FACT

Very forceful vomiting may break blood vessels in your esophagus.

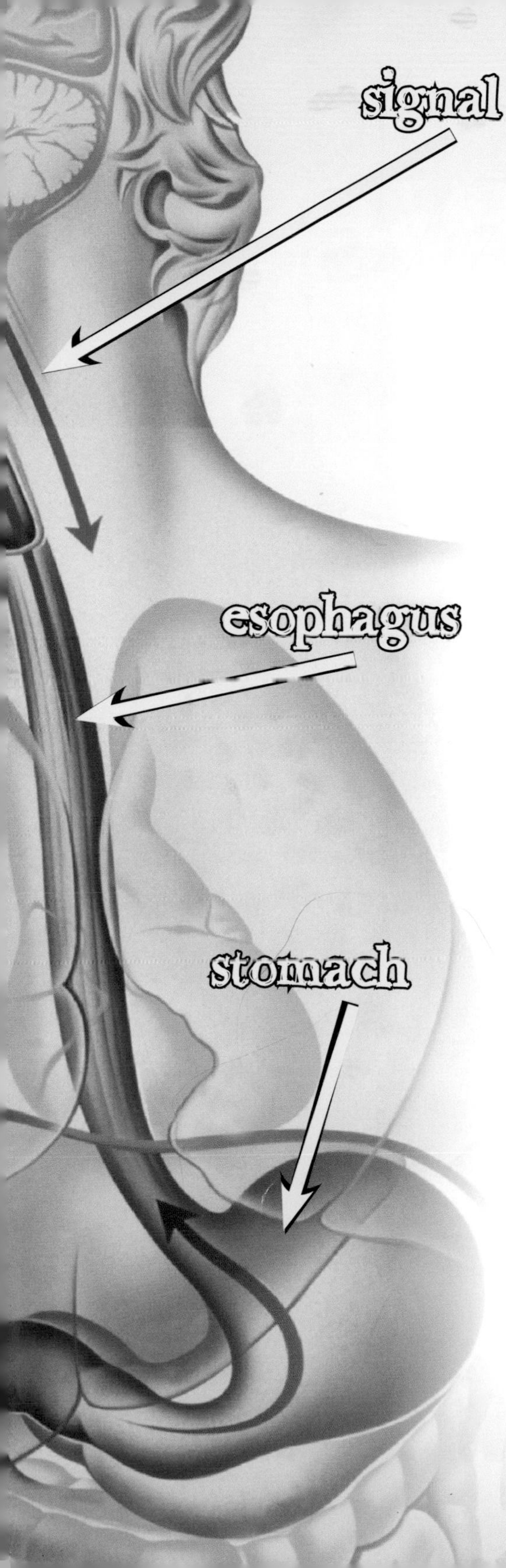

signal from brain

esophagus

stomach

First, your body makes more spit, or saliva. Spit protects your teeth from the acid that's about to come up. Next, your windpipe closes so that vomit won't get into your lungs. Then the muscles around your stomach squeeze tight. That big squeeze forces whatever is in your small intestine and your stomach back up your throat. You have to let that vomit out somehow. So, ready or not, here it comes — right out your mouth!

WHY we VOMIT

When your stomach isn't feeling well, it's a good idea to have a container nearby, just in case.

Now you know what barf is made of and how your body pushes it out. But you might still be wondering why you throw up.

MAKE ME SICK

Most of the time, it's simple. You vomit when something is bugging your stomach.

When you have an illness, you often have a **virus**. In fact, the stomach "flu" is not influenza at all. It's usually a virus that upsets the lining of your stomach and makes you barf.

People also throw up when a kind of poison, or **toxin**, is in their system. This type of illness is called food poisoning. In this case, puking could keep you from getting very ill. It might even save your life. Toxins can attack your organs and cause death. What better way to get rid of them than a forceful emptying of the stomach?

virus — a tiny particle that infects living things and causes diseases

toxin — a poisonous substance produced by a living thing

GAG REFLEX

Do you know anyone who gags when they get their teeth cleaned at the dentist? These people have a very touchy gag reflex.

The gag reflex is an automatic action that prevents you from choking on your food. Normally, when food touches the back of your throat, it's small and chewed up, and you swallow it. But if something is too large to swallow, you gag. Gagging pushes whatever has touched your throat back into your mouth so you don't choke.

People with an overly sensitive gag reflex may puke when a dentist looks at their teeth. Some people even barf when they're brushing their teeth. They'll probably have to brush them again after puking!

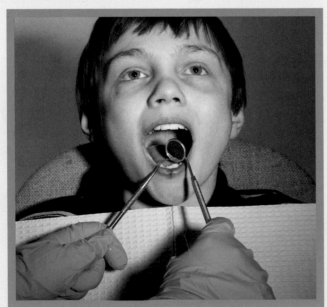

TRUST YOUR TUMMY

Some people barf when they eat too much. Your stomach can hold about 1 quart (.9 liter) of food before it's officially full. Most people stop eating when they feel full.

Holding your stomach is a common reaction to feeling nauseous.

So what happens if you keep shoving food in? Maybe you're in a pie-eating contest. Or maybe you just really like your grandma's peanut butter cookies. But if you keep eating, your stomach won't be able to keep up. Once it's too full, it will send the extra food back up.

Getting rid of all that food empties your stomach so it can feel comfortable again. In this case, barfing is your body's way of saying, "Enough is enough."

When you eat really fast, it can be difficult to know when your stomach is full.

PUKE MACHINE

Why do some babies seem to be constantly puking? You can't even look at them without sour white ooze spurting from their mouths. Baby puke may not look or smell like regular puke, but it's still gross.

A baby's only food is milk. When sucking in her supper, she can't help but get some air in her tummy. But when a baby burps, her dinner often comes up with the air. This is because her digestive muscles are weak. As the baby grows, her muscles will be able to push air out, but keep food down. Until then, keep a burp cloth handy, or just stay out of puking range!

THE NOSE KNOWS

Your sense of smell can trigger a hurl as well. When your body smells something especially nasty, it puts up its defenses. Whatever that nasty smell is coming from could have toxins in it. Your body makes you puke just in case any of those toxins got inside.

Different nerves in your nose detect a variety of scents.

If you get nervous speaking in front of others, try looking at the tops of people's heads while you speak.

MIND OVER MATTER

Sometimes people barf when they're nervous. Nothing is really wrong with your stomach when you throw up because of nerves. It's all in your mind.

President George H. W. Bush threw up on TV.
He wasn't nervous, though. He had a virus.

When you're really nervous, your brain sends signals all over your body. Some people's hands shake. Some people shiver or sweat. And some unlucky people, well, they hurl. The best way to prevent this kind of puking is to try to calm down. Breathe deeply, and relax.

Swallowing ginger tablets may help calm your stomach if you get seasick.

MOTION SICKNESS

Some people feel sick when they ride in cars, airplanes, boats, or other vehicles. They may feel dizzy, nauseous, and sweaty. This feeling is called motion sickness.

Motion sickness actually starts in your ears. Your ears consist of an outer, middle, and inner ear. The inner ear is the part of your body that gives you your sense of balance.

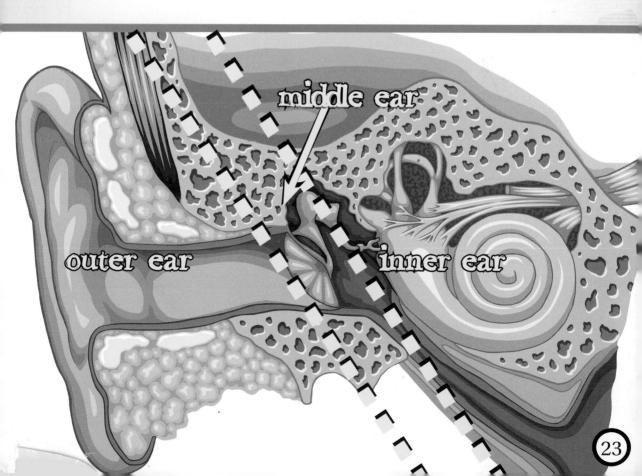

middle ear

outer ear

inner ear

Most of the time, your ears, eyes, and brain work together when you move. But sometimes something else moves your body, like a car or a ride at the amusement park. Other times your body feels like it's moving when it's not, like when you watch an action movie. In these cases, your ears, eyes, and brain can get confused. Your ears sense a shift in movement, but your eyes don't. Or your eyes sense movement, but your ears don't. This confusion can make you feel nauseous and — you guessed it — barf!

Luckily, there are ways to prevent motion sickness. If you're at least 13 years old, you can sit in the front seat of cars. Looking out the front window instead of the side windows helps your eyes and ears know what's going on. In a plane, you should take a window seat by the wing. You should also avoid playing video games or reading while moving. These tricks will help your ears and eyes understand how you're moving.

If you still feel queasy in the front seat, try sucking on a peppermint. It may help calm your stomach.

When caring for a sick friend, look away before he vomits, or you might be puking next.

Almost everyone agrees that vomit is extremely disgusting. If your stomach can handle it, read on for some of the grossest facts about barf.

IT'S A GROUP THING

Some people throw up after seeing someone else's vomit. Scientists have studied this reaction, and most agree that there is a good reason for it.

To explain, let's go back to ancient times when people lived together in big groups. They ate the same foods. They drank the same water. If one person was vomiting, there was a good chance that more of them might soon become ill. So nature protected us with a handy preventative measure. It gave us the reflex to vomit when we see other people puking. This reflex gives our bodies the ability to get rid of whatever might have made that first person sick.

THE STINK

Another gross aspect of vomit is its smell. But before you barf just thinking about it, consider this. Vomit's gross smell serves a purpose. Animals leave it alone.

It's not uncommon for a hungry animal to try to eat the waste matter of other animals. But eating vomit could make the animal very sick. Barf's awful stink keeps animals away.

THE LAST WORD

Vomit is undeniably gross. But without it, toxins and germs could roam through your body for weeks. Some animals can't vomit and may die as a result. We need to vomit to stay healthy. Think of it as a way to clean the pipes of your digestive system.

Mice, rats, and horses can't vomit. Their digestive systems don't allow it.

GLOSSARY

acid (A-suhd) — a strong liquid; stomach acids help break down food for energy.

bile (BILE) — a green liquid that is made by the liver and helps digest food

churn (CHUHRN) — to move roughly; when your stomach churns it makes you feel sick.

enzyme (EN-zime) — a substance that helps break down food

intestine (in-TESS-tin) — a long tube extending below the stomach that digests food and absorbs liquids and salts; humans have a small intestine and a large intestine.

nausea (NAW-zee-uh) — a feeling of sickness in the stomach

reflex (REE-fleks) — an action that happens without a person's control or effort

toxin (TOK-sin) — a poisonous substance produced by a living thing

virus (VYE-ruhss) — a tiny particle that infects living things and causes diseases

READ MORE

Cobb, Vicki. *Your Body Battles a Stomachache.* Body Battles. Minneapolis: Millbrook Press, 2009.

Murray, Julie. *The Body.* That's Gross! A Look at Science. Edina, Minn.: ABDO, 2009.

Szpirglas, Jeff. *Gross Universe: Your Guide to All Disgusting Things Under the Sun.* Toronto: Maple Tree Press, 2005.

INTERNET SITES

FactHound offers a safe, fun way to find Internet sites related to this book. All of the sites on FactHound have been researched by our staff.

Here's all you do:

Visit *www.facthound.com*

FactHound will fetch the best sites for you!

INDEX